PowerKiDS
Readers

Fun Fish
Peces divertidos

JELLYFISH
LAS MEDUSAS

Maddie Gibbs

Traducción al español: Eida de la Vega

PowerKiDS press.

New York

Published in 2014 by The Rosen Publishing Group, Inc.
29 East 21st Street, New York, NY 10010

First Edition

Editor: Amelie von Zumbusch
Book Design: Andrew Povolny

Traducción al español: Eida de la Vega

Photo Credits: Cover Andaman/Shutterstock.com; p. 5 Vilainecrevette/Shutterstock.com; p. 7 bluehand/Shutterstock.com; p. 9 Joe Drivas/Photographer's Choice/Getty Images; pp. 11, 13 iStockphoto/Thinkstock; p. 15 Stephan Kerkhofs/Shutterstock.com; p. 17 Levent Konuk/Shutterstock.com; p. 19 Edwin Verin/Shutterstock.com; p. 21 Henglein and Steets/Cultura/Getty Images; p. 23 Federic Pacorel/Photographer's Choice/Getty Images.

Library of Congress Cataloging-in-Publication Data

Gibbs, Maddie.
 [Jellyfish. Spanish & English]
 Jellyfish = Las medusas / by Maddie Gibbs ; translator, Eduardo Alamán. — 1st ed.
     p. cm. – (Powerkids readers. Fun fish = Peces divertidos)
 In English and Spanish.
 Includes bibliographical references and index.
 ISBN 978-1-4777-1217-7 (library binding)
 1. Jellyfishes—Juvenile literature. I. Alamán, Eduardo. II. Title. III. Title: Medusas.
 QL375.6.G5318 2014
 593.5'3—dc23
                                    2012049059

Websites: Due to the changing nature of Internet links, PowerKids Press has developed an online list of websites related to the subject of this book. This site is updated regularly. Please use this link to access the list: www.powerkidslinks.com/pkrff/jelly/

Manufactured in the United States of America

CPSIA Compliance Information: Batch #S13PK4: For Further Information contact Rosen Publishing, New York, New York at 1-800-237-9932

Contents

Contenido

Jellyfish live in seas.

Las **medusas** viven en el mar.

They have for over 500 million years!

¡Han vivido ahí por más de 500 millones de años!

They are not true fish.

En realidad, las medusas no son peces.

They have no blood, bones, or brain.

___

No tienen sangre, huesos ni cerebro.

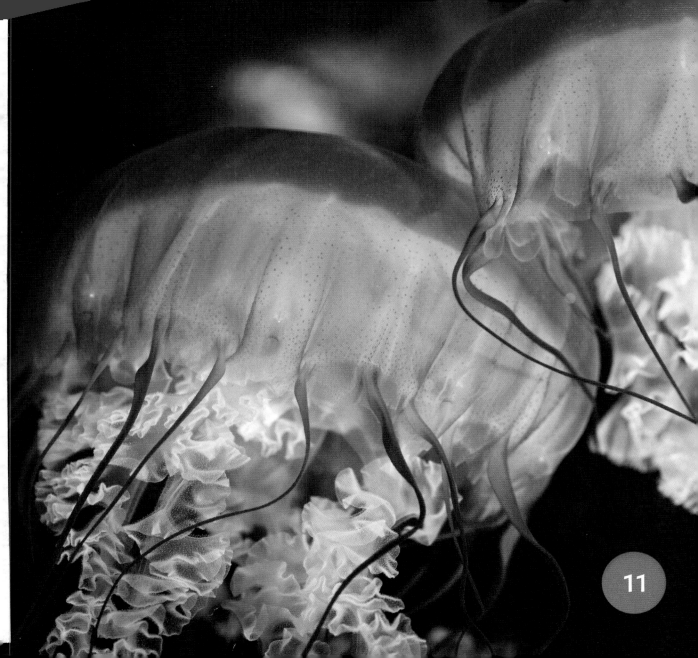

11

They **drift**.

Las medusas **van a la deriva**.

They are 95% water.

El 95% de su cuerpo es agua.

15

There are about 200 kinds.

Hay cerca de 200 tipos
de medusas.

17

A group is a **smack**.

Un grupo se llama **colonia**.

Have you seen any?

¿Has visto alguna medusa?

Take care. They can sting!

¡Cuidado! Te pueden picar.

23

WORDS TO KNOW / PALABRAS QUE DEBES SABER

drift

ir a la deriva

jellyfish

medusa

smack

colonia

INDEX

ÍNDICE